WORLD MYTHS AND LEGENDS

Regional American

Joanne Suter

Farmington River Regional Elem School
Farmington River Elementary Library
555 North Main Road
Otis, Massachusetts 01253-0679

Fearon/Janus
Belmont, CA

Simon & Schuster Supplementary Education Group

World Myths and Legends

Greek and Roman
Ancient Middle Eastern
Norse
African
Far Eastern
Celtic
Native American
Regional American

Series Editor: Joseph T. Curran
Cover Designer: Dianne Platner
Text Designer: Teresa A. Holden
Interior Illustrations: James McConnell
Cover Photo: The Granger Collection, New York

Copyright © 1992 by Fearon/Janus, 500 Harbor Blvd., Belmont, CA 94002. All rights reserved. No part of this book may be reproduced by any means, transmitted, or translated into a machine language without written permission from the publisher.

Library of Congress Catalog Card Number: 91-72591

ISBN 0-8224-4641-3

Printed in the United States of America

9 8 7 6 5 4

CONTENTS

An Introduction to Regional American Folklore

1 Legendary Heroes

Davy Crockett	1
Johnny Appleseed	6
Felipa	13
Mike Fink	22
Annie Christmas	28
Febold Feboldson	33
Pecos Bill	41
Paul Bunyan	50
John Henry	60

2 Rebels and Rascals

Blackbeard	68
Jean Lafitte	73
Jesse James	80

3 Regional Favorites

Rip Van Winkle	87
The Witches of Windham	95
Flight	99
The Jumping Frog	103

Pronunciation Guide   107

An Introduction to Regional American Folklore

This is a collection of tales from the United States. Another book in this series, *Native American Myths and Legends,* presents the stories of the first Americans. This book presents the folklore of the country's immigrants and their descendants.

Folklore reflects peoples' customs and beliefs. Stories told by settlers reflect both the settlers' origins and the characteristics of the places they settle. These vary from region to region. In New Mexico, for example, the settlers were mostly of Mexican or Spanish heritage. They lived in the high desert. Their stories are quite different from those of the British who settled around Massachusetts Bay.

Folklore is usually passed from one generation to the next by word of mouth. It is part of an oral tradition of story telling. This book expands on that process by including stories that are part of America's written literature.

Many of the people you'll read about in this book were heroes. Their stories are sometimes called "tall tales" because they contain greatly exaggerated details. But often the stories are based on the lives of real people. Many stories describe qualities that are often thought to be particularly American. These include strength, self-confidence, hearty good humor, and persistence. Notice that most of the folk heroes are not from the upper social classes. They are mainly workers. This emphasizes the belief that in America, any man or woman can act heroically.

Most American folklore is very positive. The tale called "Flight" finds hope in the midst of despair. Stories of Jean Lafitte and Jesse James point out the good in the hearts of legendary villains. Faith and strength prevail in the character of Felipa, a woman who wouldn't give up. In "The Witches of Windham" and "The Jumping Frog," Americans were able to laugh at themselves.

This society is a blend of many languages, religions, and cultures. Our folklore reflects the differences. Yet it also reflects common themes and ideas that make it uniquely American.

Davy Crockett

Davy Crockett was a hunter, soldier, and politician. He guided U.S. troops into unknown lands. And he joined the Texas struggle for independence from Mexico. In 1836, he was killed at the battle of the Alamo.

Frontier tale-tellers loved to spin yarns about Crockett that turned him into a larger-than-life figure. It was said that he could "run faster, jump higher, squat lower, dive deeper, stay under longer, and come out drier than any man in the whole country."

Young Davy

Davy Crockett was born in Hawkins County, Tennessee. "Come, look here!" the neighbors cried on the day of his birth. The infant was the largest baby anyone in those parts had ever seen. Indeed, that boy grew up fast, drinking buffalo milk and whiskey. When Davy lost his baby teeth, his family used them to build the fireplace in their parlor. By his eighth birthday, Davy weighed 200 pounds. And that was with his shoes off and his stomach empty!

Young Davy wasn't keen on book-learning. After his fourth day of school, he ran away from home. Davy took well to life on his own. In just eight months, he killed 105 bears.

By the time he was fully grown, Davy had made a name for himself among both men and beasts. Some animals would lie right down and die when Davy grinned at them. Others, looking down from a tree and seeing him reach for his gun, would holler, "Is that you, Davy? Don't shoot! I'm coming down!"

Once Davy chased a bear up a tree. When he couldn't grab hold of the bear with his hands, Davy bit into the bear's tail. The bear kept climbing, pulling Davy up the tree behind him. At the top of the tree, they both fell. Davy hit the ground, grabbed his rifle, and was ready to shoot. But the bear ran off, squealing from the pain in his rear end.

Davy had only one thing to say about the experience: "I'd like to have thanked that bear, for he did me a service. I'd had a bit of a toothache, and biting his tail cured me entirely. I've never had any pain since. I recommend that anyone with a toothache chew on two inches of bear's tail. It's a certain cure!"

Davy Crockett

1. What did Davy's parents make with his baby teeth?
2. How many bears did Davy kill in eight months?
3. How did Davy cure his toothache?

The Politician

Davy was poor and uneducated. He didn't learn to read until he was 18. But the frontier people thought he had good sense. "He's got horse-sense!" they said. In 1827, they elected him to Congress.

Davy loved talking to crowds, and he had a quick wit. By his own description, he was a fine "speechifier." Once on the campaign trail, a man running against Davy was getting the best of him in a debate. Then some hens outside the meeting hall started making a terrible racket.

"Listen!" Davy cried. "Even those hens over there are calling my name!" Indeed, the squawking did sound like "Crockett." The audience roared with laughter, and they never forgot his name.

4. How old was Davy when he learned to read?
5. When was Davy Crockett elected to Congress?
6. Why did the people at the debate never forget his name?

After the Alamo

Now history tells us that Davy met his death at the Alamo. But there are stories to the contrary. Some folks say he gave the Mexican army an awful licking and then rode south on the back of his tame bear, Death Hug. According to those accounts, Davy Crockett was still alive and kicking.

7. Why did Davy run away from home?
8. What did the frontier people mean by "horse-sense"?
9. Where did Davy Crockett die?

Johnny Appleseed

Johnny Appleseed was a gentle American hero whose real name was John Chapman. Beginning at the age of 23, he spent 48 years traveling between Pennsylvania and Indiana, planting apple orchards. He preached kindness and love of all living things. Johnny Appleseed was a legend in his own time. But stories of his adventures are still told today.

The Apple Man

The settlers knew him as Johnny Appleseed, a strange fellow who planted apple seeds wherever he went.

When Johnny was a young man, he had left his home in Massachusetts and moved to Pennsylvania. There he had a vision one night.

"Go west," said the angels in his dream. They showed him a heavenly city that was surrounded by fruit trees laden with sweet blossoms. "Plant your seeds so that the wilderness might bloom like this heavenly city."

Now Johnny was a religious man, and he didn't question the angels' words. He filled a leather sack with apple seeds and made his way westward.

When he met up with settlers, Johnny planted his seeds and told the settlers how to tend the young trees. He took no money for his seeds or advice.

The settlers soon came to recognize this odd character. Of course, he was hard to miss. For a shirt, Johnny wore an old burlap coffee sack with holes cut out for his arms and head. Over his long dark hair he wore a tin pot that he also used for cooking. Johnny's feet were bare, for he liked the feel of the earth.

"He's light in the head!" some people exclaimed.

"He's the kindest fellow you'd ever want to meet!" said others.

Most nights, Johnny made his camp under the stars. When the weather turned bitterly cold, he slept in barns.

1. *Where was Johnny Appleseed born?*
2. *Why did Johnny decide to travel west planting apple seeds?*
3. *Why were Johnny's feet bare?*

Johnny and the Animals

Johnny had a close relationship with the creatures of the wilderness. People often saw him talking aloud to birds and squirrels. He and a bear once took their evening's rest together in a hollow log.

And Johnny loved the smallest creatures as well. One cool night he built a campfire and settled down to cook his supper. He noticed that tiny mosquitoes were attracted to the flame. He watched with distress as they flew into the fire and were burned. Johnny immediately put out his campfire to spare the insects' lives. He happily ate his dinner cold.

One day when Johnny was tramping through the woods, he heard a terrible snarling. He turned and saw a large black wolf. The wolf growled at Johnny and showed him his sharp teeth. But as Johnny drew closer, he saw that the animal's foot was caught in a steel trap.

"Don't be afraid, Brother Wolf," Johnny whispered. And though the wolf growled a bit, it let Johnny remove its leg from the trap. Then Johnny bandaged the wolf's wound and gently stroked its dark pointed ears.

Johnny Appleseed

Johnny stayed beside the wolf for several days. He changed its bandage, brought it water, and waited for the wound to heal. When the wolf was well, Johnny started off on his travels again. And the wolf padded along behind him.

4. *What animal once shared a hollow log with Johnny?*
5. *Why did Johnny eat his dinner cold?*
6. *What did Johnny do to help the wolf?*

Johnny and the Battle of Tippecanoe

Now Johnny hated bloodshed and didn't believe in fighting. But when the Battle of Tippecanoe broke out, Johnny was there. He ran about on the battlefield, dragging the wounded off to safety. It didn't matter to him which side a man might be fighting on. He helped whoever was in need.

It was at Tippecanoe that two bullets slammed into Johnny's chest. But they didn't stop him. The bullets had struck the Bible he always carried close to his heart.

When the battle was over, Johnny took out the Bible and found the bullets stuck in its cover. "You can always count on the Good Book," he said.

7. Who did Johnny drag off the battlefield?
8. What slammed into Johnny's chest?
9. What protected Johnny from being hurt?

Johnny's Work Is Done

As the frontier moved westward, so did Johnny Appleseed. He'd travel on when he saw towns and apple orchards spring up around him.

"I've got a pack on my back and seeds in my sack," sang Johnny. "My seeds I shall sow, wherever I go. Then the Lord comes along with his rain and his sun, and that's when I know that my day's work is done."

It was in an orchard that a traveler found the body of old Johnny Appleseed. He was still dressed in a burlap sack and was still wearing a tin pot on his head. Around him stood a circle of wild animals. There was a peaceful smile on his face. Overhead, sweet-scented blooms blew gently in the morning breeze.

To this very day, folks point out trees that they say grew from seeds planted by Johnny Appleseed.

10. Where did a traveler find Johnny Appleseed's body?
11. Who else was there?
12. What sort of expression was on Johnny's face when he died?

Felipa

From New Mexico comes this tale of a heroine named Felipa. It is the story of a woman whose courage and independence brought about a miracle.

A Woman Alone

Long ago the Spaniards journeyed north from Mexico looking for gold. They came to a high desert that was blooming with flowers and strange cacti. They called it New Mexico. The Spaniards found villages built into the walls of cliffs. The people who lived in the villages were of the Pueblo tribe. They were peaceful farmers. They weren't prepared to fight the Spaniards, who soon took their land and brought them under their rule.

The Utes also lived in New Mexico. The Utes were warriors. They planted no crops but stole food and animals from others. The Utes often raided Pueblo villages. When the Spaniards arrived, the Utes attacked their settlements too.

The Spaniards built low, flat houses out of mud bricks called *adobe*. In one of these adobe houses lived a beautiful young woman named Felipa. She had a handsome husband and a seven-year-old son. They lived together happily, tending their garden and fields.

But one day the Utes rode into their village. Their painted faces were frightening, and they waved weapons over their heads. They stole what they could, and murdered those who got in their way. They killed Felipa's husband as he stood in the yard in front of their home. And one Ute warrior swept up Felipa's little son and carried him away on his horse. Felipa ran screaming from her house and chased after the raiding party. But it quickly disappeared from sight.

Felipa wept over her husband's body and wailed for her lost child.

Though her heart was broken, Felipa bravely went on with her life. She was determined to keep her home and her fields. Working alone, she soon harvested a very fine crop.

The people of the village admired this strong young woman. They felt her sorrow and did what they could to help her. Neighbors often left bundles of firewood at her door.

There was one man in the village,

however, whose heart was cold. His name was José, and his flock of sheep was the largest for miles around.

Every day José passed Felipa's house as he drove his sheep to pasture. "What a lovely woman!" he whispered under his breath. He decided he would have her for his wife.

But Felipa's heart was still full of love for her husband and son. When José asked her to marry him, she said no.

José was furious. He was a rich and powerful man. How dare she refuse him? He angrily drove his sheep right through Felipa's fields.

"Stop!" Felipa cried. "Take your herds away. All my hard work will be ruined!"

José sat on his horse and laughed as his sheep destroyed Felipa's crops.

Now Felipa was a gentle soul, but this was too much! "May Saint Cristobal meet you on your way home," she shouted angrily. "May he throw you over the cliff, and may you break your neck!"

José turned and rode off, his laughter echoing behind him.

Later that day, the news reached Felipa. José's horse had been climbing a steep trail up a cliff. Suddenly it lost its footing. José toppled over the edge of the cliff. He died of a broken neck.

1. *Who killed Felipa's husband and took her child?*
2. *What did Felipa's neighbors often leave at her door?*
3. *Why did José let his sheep ruin Felipa's crops?*

Felipa's Task

When Felipa heard this, she broke into sobs. Had the blessed Saint Cristobal heard her? Had Felipa caused José's death?

Felipa ran to the church and knelt before the altar. All night long she prayed for forgiveness. And all night long the angry face of José seemed to stare at her from out of the darkness.

In the morning, the priest came into the church. Felipa told him her story.

"Help me, good Father," she begged. "Give me some task to do so that I might earn forgiveness."

"No person can bring about another's death simply by wishing it," the priest said. "But you acted wrongly, and therefore, I will give you a task."

Felipa

"When José was alive, he did little for others. Perhaps in his death, some good can be done. Take José's herd of sheep and travel the land. Whenever you find someone in need, give that person one of the sheep. Give it in the name of José and with the blessing of Saint Cristobal. And pray to Saint Cristobal every morning and evening. If he is pleased, he will give you a sign at the end of your task. He will make you very, very happy!"

Felipa had little hope of happiness. Since her son had been stolen, she had resigned herself to sorrow. But she heeded the priest's instructions and set out with José's sheep. Felipa went from village to village, finding many people in need of help. They were all very grateful when the kind young woman gave them a healthy sheep.

Each morning and evening Felipa prayed to Saint Cristobal. And each night she dreamed of José's face. But it seemed that with each sheep Felipa gave away, his face looked less angry and more content.

As Felipa traveled, one sheep took to walking beside her. It was a large black ewe, which she named Negrita. Negrita nuzzled Felipa's hand when it was time to eat and slept near her side at night.

Felipa grew to love that ewe.

At last Felipa had given away all the herd except Negrita. Although she loved the animal, Felipa's task would not be complete until every sheep had a new home. Felipa walked on, but could find no one who needed Negrita.

Far out in the country, Felipa came upon a tumbled-down one-room hut made of stones and mud. In front of the hut stood a tall, shabbily dressed man. He was leaning on a staff.

"My friend," called Felipa, "you look like you could use a little help. May I give you this sheep?"

The man shook his head no. Felipa noticed that he had very kind eyes. "I am strong," he said, "and I can make my own way in this world. However, there is someone in my hut to whom you may give your sheep. I found him only yesterday when I visited a Navajo village. The Navajo had traded for him with the Utes, who stole him from a Spanish village. They sold him to me for a piece of turquoise."

Felipa ran to the door of the hut. In the room's dim light, she saw a small figure. She knew immediately that it was her own son. Felipa rushed forward to hold him in her arms.

Laughing and crying, she turned to thank the man. But he was neither in the hut nor in the yard. He had completely disappeared.

Felipa took her son's hand. With Negrita following behind them, they walked back toward their village. Felipa asked all those she passed if they had seen a tall man with a staff. But no one remembered such a fellow. In fact, when she mentioned the little hut, they said it had been deserted for years.

By the time she reached home, Felipa knew what had happened. The man she had met was Saint Cristobal himself. He had smiled upon her and given her back her child. This is what the priest had meant when he said Saint Cristobal would make her happy.

That night Felipa's house seemed full again, for her son lay safe in his bed. And that night she dreamed of José for the last time. His face was bright and smiling. Felipa's good deeds had brought him peace.

4. What happened every time Felipa gave away a sheep?
5. Which of the sheep was Felipa's favorite?
6. Who did the tall, shabbily dressed man turn out to be?

Mike Fink

> Storytelling was once a favorite pastime across the United States. Storytellers held contests to see who could create the best tale. To impress their listeners, they created heroes who could perform fantastic feats. The stories of these heroes became America's tall tales.
>
> One of these "tall tale" heroes was Mike Fink, who ran a keelboat on the Mississippi and Ohio rivers. Keelboats were shallow covered boats that were used to carry people and goods down the rivers. The keelboats had no engines. They had to be pushed and pulled back upstream by hand. The keelboatmen were a rough and ready group. Legend says the best of them all was Mike Fink.

The River Roarer

"I'm a river roarer! I'm a ringtailed squealer! I'm a regular screamer from the old Mississip'! I'm half wild horse and half alligator! I can outrun, outjump, outshoot, outfight, and outbrag any man! I can shoot the scales off a leaping trout! I can straighten the curl in a pig's tail from 50 feet away!"

Barrel-chested Mike Fink was roaring his boasts from the top of a barroom table. He'd spent the day poling his keelboat upstream against the current. Now he and his crew were in town for some fun. And to Mike, that meant bragging and shooting and fighting.

There was nothing Mike Fink liked better than a good fight. But he wasn't a mean sort. Not at all. In fact, the man he most liked wrestling with was his best pal Carpenter, another keelboatman. It was all in fun, Mike would say. And he always shook his opponent's hand when the tumble was over.

"Now don't disappoint me, boys!" Mike crowed. "I'm ready for a fight!"

Though Mike wasn't very tall, he was tough as a bale of barbed wire and strong as dynamite. The red feather he wore in his hat was the badge of the toughest keelboatman. No one in the bar was eager to take him on.

So Mike had to content himself with drinking and singing and telling tall tales of life on the river. It wasn't until early the next morning that he got himself into a good fight.

1. What did Mike Fink do for a living?
2. What did he like better than anything?
3. What did the red feather in Mike's hat mean?

The Outlaws

Shortly before dawn, when the sky was still dark and the river quiet, outlaws climbed aboard Mike's keelboat.

Mike had been sleeping with one eye open. He had his six-foot rifle, which he called Bang-All, by his side. Mike heard those pirates steal aboard and rustle through his cargo. They were there only moments before Mike and his men were out of their beds.

"All right!" Mike shouted. "A fight at last!" In the darkness, Mike saw 10 or 12 robbers at the bow of his boat. He and his crew rushed forward. They were outnumbered, but that only made the fight more interesting.

"Down you go!" Mike cried as he punched out one man after another.

When the last pirate was thrown into the river, Mike shouted, "That's the end of robbing keelboats for you!" Mike was happy. He loved putting such rascals in their place.

4. When did the pirates climb aboard Mike's keelboat?
5. What did Mike call his rifle?
6. Why didn't Mike and his men worry about being outnumbered?

Shooting the Cup

One of Mike Fink's other favorite activities was playing a game called "shoot the cup." First he would fill a tin cup just about full to the brim with cider. Then he would place the cup on top of his friend Carpenter's head.

Mike would stand back about 60 yards and take aim with Bang-All. Then he'd shoot right through the rim of the cup without spilling a drop of cider. Sometimes Carpenter would shoot a cup on Mike's head, but he'd usually spill the cider.

After performing this trick for a crowd, Mike and Carpenter would laugh loudly and take a bow. The two were the best of friends, and they often swore they were ready to die for each other.

Mississippi steamboat

Such a pair they were, that indeed it seemed no one could ever defeat them. But one man did put a very dark shadow over their lives. Now this man wasn't big or strong, and he didn't whoop and holler. His name was Robert Fulton, and he was the inventor of the steamboat.

Mike Fink hated steamboats. Every time he saw a big wheel churning up the water, he'd stomp his feet and shake his fist at the sky. The steamboats took away a lot of Mike's business. Before very long, it was Fulton, not Mike, that folks were calling king of the river. In time, Mike and Carpenter started talking about leaving the Mississippi and heading west.

They planned on having many more

good times together. But one day they had a quarrel. No one knows what they argued about. And everyone swears they made up and shook hands. But later something went terribly wrong.

Mike and Carpenter were putting on a show. Mike handed Carpenter the tin cup full of cider, and Carpenter placed it on his head. Some folks say Carpenter was still shaky from the argument. Others are sure the sunlight made Mike blink. But one thing's for sure. When Mike fired his gun, he put a bullet straight through Carpenter's forehead. His friend fell dead.

"Well," said a spectator, "I guess you're not such a great shot after all."

"I *am* a good shot!" Mike said. "I . . ."

Mike never finished that sentence. Another friend of Carpenter's had taken out his own gun. He pointed it at Mike and shot him in the heart.

Mike was buried wearing the hat with the red feather stuck in it.

7. *How did Mike and his friend Carpenter play "shoot the cup"?*
8. *Why didn't Mike like Robert Fulton?*
9. *What happened to Mike?*

Annie Christmas

> *Some stories say that Annie Christmas was white, but most describe her as a black woman. They all agree that she was the strongest woman in all of Louisiana.*

Annie Christmas worked on the Mississippi River between New Orleans and Natchez. Like Mike Fink, she hauled keelboats upriver against the current. Annie was nearly seven feet tall, and she weighed over 250 pounds. She had a dark mustache and usually wore men's clothing.

Annie would fight other keelboaters a dozen at a time. She'd lick 'em, too. Some folks say Mike Fink himself never came into town when Annie was there. They say he was afraid of standing up to her.

Now Annie sometimes tired of her rough-and-tumble life. On those occasions, she'd shave off her mustache and scrub her skin with sweet-smelling soap. She'd dress in red satin, place scarlet feathers in her hair, and put on a long beaded necklace.

Then Annie would go out looking for a man. One night she met a certain riverboat captain and decided to take a ride on the

Annie Christmas

man's paddle-wheeler. She climbed aboard the paddle-wheeler and tied up her keelboat to its stern.

She and the captain had a fine time until the weather got rough. Storm clouds appeared overhead, and water rose in swells around the boat. Annie was reminded of the saying that the devil and the Mississippi are first cousins.

The captain of the paddle-wheeler had a hard time staying on course. He began swearing. Annie stood nearby with her scarlet feathers blowing in the wind. She didn't say a word.

As the winds blew harder, the captain grew angrier. He cursed the wind and water and blamed the devil for his trouble. Now there was nothing Annie hated more than evil-tempered men. At last she said, "Hold your tongue! If you don't stop calling the devil, he'll come here and fetch you!"

"Let him!" the captain roared. "I wish he'd take the whole Mississippi!"

"Did you hear that, devil?" screamed Annie. Now, she wasn't about to hang around waiting for the devil to snatch her. So she quickly jumped aboard her keelboat and pushed off from the paddle-wheeler into the swirling river.

"Captain, I'm afraid you'll get your wish!" she yelled as she poled for shore. When Annie reached land, she tied the keelboat's rope around her waist. Running in long strides, she towed that keelboat all the way to New Orleans.

As for the captain, he was never seen again. But folks who live by the river claim that on stormy nights they hear his paddle-wheeler churning the water. They also say they hear the captain swearing in the darkness to the devil.

Annie Christmas remained strong and hardy all the rest of her days. But her time did come, as it does to even the greatest of heroes. When Annie died, the entire city of New Orleans came out to bid her farewell.

Annie had 12 fine sons, and each was as tall and strong as she was. Annie's sons had her dressed for her funeral in a black satin gown. Then they carried her coffin to the river. There a great crowd had gathered.

They watched as the coffin was placed on a waiting barge. When Annie's sons stepped back from the barge, it mysteriously began to move. There was nothing on board but the coffin. There was no person or thing to power the boat. But everyone saw it float slowly from sight.

It could be that Annie is still sailing the Mississippi. Some people say they've seen her barge on lonely, moonless nights.

1. *How big was Annie Christmas?*
2. *Why did Annie get off the captain's paddle-wheeler?*
3. *Where did Annie's 12 sons put her body when she died? What happened to it?*

Febold Feboldson

In the 19th century, explorers, pioneers, and gold rushers bound for Oregon and California traveled across America. Settlers at first showed little interest in the vast Great Plains in the middle of the country. They thought nothing would grow there. The weather was said to be either too hot or too cold, either too wet or too dry. But the soil was in fact fertile.

In 1862, the U.S. Government passed the Homestead Act. It promised 160 acres of land to anyone who would settle it.

Homesteaders' stories pointed out how tough and unpredictable their lives on the plains were. Febold Feboldson was a character who could overcome all the difficulties.

Febold's Great Idea

The first European to settle in Nebraska was a Swedish man named Febold Feboldson.

Back in 1849, people were rushing across the country to get to the gold fields of California. They were looking for a quick way to get rich. Febold Feboldson drove a team of oxen that pulled a train of prairie schooners. Febold's canvas-covered wagons carried folks over the plains and mountains all the way from Kansas City, Kansas, to California.

But in the winter of '49, a terrible storm blew in from the north. It snowed for months on end. When spring came, the snow didn't melt. It just sat there on the ground. By summer, it had turned to stone. That August, the temperature never rose higher than 100 degrees below zero. The plains were hard as marble. Febold couldn't get a single customer to venture across them with him.

Now Febold was a man of ideas. "Nothing's impossible!" he always used to say. So Febold sat down and started thinking. What he needed was heat. People would travel across the plains if they could keep warm enough. And where could you find heat? Why, in the desert, of course.

Febold headed for the hottest desert he knew of—Death Valley, in California. There he loaded each of his wagons with burning sand that he brought back to Kansas City.

"Get your sand!" Febold shouted. "Hot

sand from the desert! Guaranteed to keep you warm all the way to California."

In no time at all Febold had sold all his sand. The gold rushers dumped it in their wagons and sat on top of it. The sand kept them warm as they traveled across the plains.

Everything went well until the wagon train reached Nebraska. The road there was quite bumpy. The wagons swayed, and much of the sand spilled out of them. So much of it scattered on the ground, in fact, that it covered all the ice.

But Febold didn't notice this until he was making his return trip from California. Passing through Nebraska again, he found the whole state sizzling with heat. The only things growing were a few gray cottonwood trees and some parched yellow buffalo grass. The rivers had turned into dried-up cracks in the earth.

"Look what I've done to Nebraska!" Febold cried out. He felt very bad. But Febold was an honest fellow, and he was always willing to correct a mistake.

So Febold gave up his wagon train and built a little house for himself. Then he started thinking of ways to get other settlers to come to Nebraska.

1. What were prairie schooners?
2. What did Febold bring that melted the ice?
3. How did Nebraska get to be sizzling with heat?

Nebraska Days

Febold looked at the buffalo grass growing out of the sand. "It would make good feed for cattle and sheep," he thought to himself. Febold wrote to all the cattle ranchers and sheepherders he knew. And soon the state was filled with ranchers, cowboys, and sheepherders.

Then Febold had another idea. He wrote to farmers and asked them to try raising grain in Nebraska. The farmers came, too.

At first those who were grazing animals didn't get along very well with those who were raising crops. The cattle and sheep tore up the farmers' fields. Things quieted down, though, after Febold helped the farmers build fences.

But even with that problem solved, Nebraska gave its settlers plenty of trouble. The wind could blow so hard that it would pluck the feathers right off the chickens. There were winters so cold that smoke froze to chimneys. Some summers got so hot that cast-iron stoves melted.

One year the weather was stranger than usual, even for Nebraska. The sun shone and the rain fell at the same time. The sun would shine on a mile-wide strip of ground. And rain would fall over the next mile-wide strip. All of Nebraska was like that—a mile of bright sunshine and then a mile of gray rain.

Now Febold's ranch was in a place where two strips met. Febold was growing corn in a valley and sugarcane on a nearby hill. Well, the sun shone so hot on that valley that the corn began to pop. It popped right off its ears and lay on the ground like snow.

At the same time, a heavy rain poured down on the hill. The rain washed the juice out of the sugarcane, and it flowed down the hill in a flood of molasses. The flood's force rolled the popcorn into huge balls. They must have been a hundred feet high.

"Say, this is pretty tasty!" said Febold as he bit into a piece of the sweetened popcorn.

Febold started thinking he could make a fortune selling popcorn balls. But just then the sky got really dark. Febold looked up and saw a swarm of grasshoppers. Soon the grasshoppers landed, and they covered

Febold's popcorn balls. The grasshoppers munched and crunched until there wasn't a kernel of popcorn left.

4. What did Febold think when he saw the buffalo grass?
5. What two crops did Febold grow that turned into popcorn balls?
6. What happened to the popcorn balls before Febold could sell them?

The Drought-Buster

Just after the grasshoppers ate all Febold's corn, the big drought came along. Folks called it the Year of the Great Heat. The sun seemed to shine hotter every day. And the soil got drier.

"This here drought has got to be busted!" cried Febold. He sat down to think about how to bring rain.

"The best way to do this is to make a lot of noise," he finally decided. "After all, it always rains right after the firecrackers are shot off on the Fourth of July. And the Indians shake rattles and beat on drums to bring rain. So I've just got to think of a way to make a big noise."

Febold thought a while longer. "Nothing makes as much noise as frogs when they all start croaking," he figured. "But they'll only croak if they know rain is coming."

So Febold got a couple of frogs and sat them down in front of him. He stared into their eyes and waved his pocket watch back and forth. Before long, those frogs were hypnotized.

"The rain is coming, the rain is coming," Febold told them.

Sure enough, the frogs believed it was about to rain. They began croaking. Then they hopped off to tell the other frogs to start croaking, too.

"The rain is coming!" they sang. "The rain is coming!" Soon every frog in Nebraska was croaking this tune.

First some wispy clouds appeared in the sky. Then the clouds got thicker and thicker. Finally the rain poured down in buckets.

When the sun came out again, the grass was turning green. The crops were coming up, and the animals were grazing happily.

Febold went on to bust drought after drought. His fame spread, and soon more and more folks decided to move to Nebraska. They did real well there, too.

7. Why did Febold think making noise would bring rain?
8. How did Febold convince the frogs it was going to rain?
9. What did Febold do once the drought was over?

Pecos Bill

> *Southwestern cowboys created a character they called Pecos Bill. Bill was large, strong, and courageous. Each tale the cowboys told about him became taller than the one before it.*

Coyote Boy

People say that Pecos Bill was the most remarkable Texan who ever lived.

Bill was unusual right from the start. As a baby, he refused to drink ordinary milk. So his mother fed him the milk of a mountain lion. Then she noticed that Bill was a lot rougher than his 16 brothers and sisters. So she brought him home a young bear for a playmate.

At first the bear didn't act very friendly toward Bill. It threatened to bite him. But Bill soon tamed the bear, and it followed him around like a puppy.

At that time, Texas was a wide-open, unsettled land. But when Bill was a year old, another family started homesteading about 50 miles away.

"It's getting too crowded around here!"

Bill's father exclaimed. He loaded the family into a wagon to move them further west.

The 17 children, the two adults, and all the family's goods bumped along until they reached the Pecos River. "We'll just have to cross it," Bill's father said.

The wagon plunged into the river. Its swift current tugged at a board on the bottom of the wagon. As the wagon bumped up onto dry land again, the board tore loose. And little Bill fell out onto the ground.

Well, with everyone squawking and the wagon bumping so loudly, no one heard Bill scream. In fact, it wasn't until four days later that someone took a nose count and noticed he was missing.

Meanwhile, Bill remained on the bank of the Pecos. He wasn't scared, but he did wonder what was going to happen to him. When Bill got very hungry, he began to wail. A mother coyote heard him crying and came out of her den to investigate.

She found Bill toddling along on the bank of the river. "What's the matter, little fellow?" she asked.

When Bill said he was hungry, the coyote told him to get up on her back. Then she carried him to her den and fed him some freshly killed rabbit meat.

The rabbit tasted good, and soon Bill was quite happy. He played with the coyote cubs as if they were his brothers and sisters. Before long, Bill learned the coyote language. He also learned to hunt and to howl at the moon. In time he forgot all about his earlier life and came to think of himself as a coyote.

One day when Bill was ten, he was loping along by himself when he ran into a cowboy. The cowboy spotted the naked boy and climbed down from his horse. When Bill saw the cowboy, he put his head down low and snarled.

"Who in thunder are you?" the startled cowboy asked.

Bill didn't know anything but coyote talk, so he couldn't answer him. The cowboy tossed Bill a plug of tobacco. Bill ate it and thought it tasted pretty good. He came up closer to the man and sniffed at him. The man smelled friendly enough, and there was something about his scent that was strangely familiar.

The cowboy stayed there with Bill for three days. He taught Bill to talk like a human. Then he tried to convince him that he wasn't a coyote.

"I must be a coyote!" Bill cried. "I've got

fleas and I howl at the moon!"

"All Texans have fleas!" said the cowboy. "Why, if you were a coyote, you'd have a bushy tail!"

Bill looked over his shoulder at his own rear end. And sure enough, the cowboy was right. Bill *didn't* have a tail. So he said good-bye to his coyote friends. He caught a mountain lion, straddled it, and rode off with the cowboy. Bill left the Pecos River behind him. But from then on, folks called him Pecos Bill.

1. What kind of milk did Pecos Bill drink as a baby?
2. Where did the mother coyote find little Bill?
3. How did Pecos Bill figure out he wasn't a coyote?

Pecos Bill Rides a Cyclone

The man took Bill to the Dusty Dipper Ranch. Young though he was, Bill quickly took over as boss of all the other cowboys. Until Pecos Bill came along, they were doing a pretty poor job of being cowboys. To catch steers, they'd put little loops of rope down on the ground. Then they'd wait for the steers to step into them.

But Bill changed everything. He showed the cowboys how to lasso steers. Then he invented ten-gallon hats, spurs, and sixguns. And he taught the cowboys how to sing and write songs.

One day, Bill found a strong wild mustang that no one, even he, could outrun. And no one but Bill could ride that horse. Those who tried ended up with broken necks. That's why Bill called the mustang Widow-Maker.

Bill stayed on at the Dusty Dipper until he had it running well. Then he and Widow-Maker set off. They traveled across the southwest helping out on cattle drives and starting new ranches.

Bill's fame soon spread across Texas, Oklahoma, New Mexico, and Arizona. Folks learned they could count on Bill in times of trouble. So when the terrible drought came, it was only natural that they would ask him to help them.

"You've got to do something, Bill," they said. "The whole country's drying up. We need rain."

Now Bill had done many wonderful things, but he had never made it rain. He climbed up on Widow-Maker and rode the

Pecos Bill

range, thinking hard. Day after day Bill watched the sky, hoping to see the tiniest cloud. And day after day, the sky remained empty and blue.

Then Bill spied something in the distance. As he rode closer he saw that it was a dark whirling funnel.

"That's a cyclone!" Bill said. "I'll just bet it holds some rain."

Bill galloped up to the cyclone, twirling his lasso over his head. He roped the twister and pulled himself aboard. Bill rode the cyclone across four states, squeezing the rain out of it.

The cyclone took Bill to California, where at last it ran out of steam. Bill tumbled to the ground. His fall scooped out thousands of acres of sand and rock. It left behind a basin that was later named Death Valley.

4. What was the name of Pecos Bill's horse?
5. Why did Bill lasso and squeeze the cyclone?
6. Where did the cyclone finally run out of steam?

Pecos Bill at Home

In time Bill got lonely and decided he wanted to marry. He met a spirited young woman called Slue-Foot Sue and asked her to be his bride.

Sue and Bill had a huge family. Besides their own kids, they raised a batch of orphaned coyotes. Those coyotes grew up so human-like that two of them were elected to the House of Representatives.

Bill grew older, of course, but he could always rope any steer or bust any bronco. He spent most of his time running his ranch, driving cattle, and ridding towns of outlaws.

We don't know for sure how Pecos Bill died. But most folks say he met his end while on a Colorado cattle drive. They say Bill had just met a dude from back east who fancied himself a cowboy. The dude wore a Stetson hat and shiny spurs. But he didn't know a horse from a dog or a rope from a rattlesnake. He asked Bill so many silly questions about cow punching that Bill just burst out laughing. He laughed and laughed and couldn't stop himself.

Now you may think this is a pretty sad way to end this story. Or you may think it's a pretty good way. But the fact is—at least as people tell it—that Pecos Bill laughed himself to death!

You can look at Bill's passing however you like. But you must admit that he was just about the greatest cowboy of them all.

7. *What was the name of Pecos Bill's wife?*
8. *What is meant by a "dude" in the story?*
9. *How do most people say that Pecos Bill died?*

Paul Bunyan

> From Maine to Oregon, lumbermen told stories of Paul Bunyan and his blue ox, Babe. Working together, these two could solve any lumber camp problem.
>
> The Paul Bunyan legend dates back to around 1860. As time went on, the tales grew more numerous and more fantastic. In 1910, some of them were printed in a Detroit newspaper. In 1922, the Red River Lumber Company used the Paul Bunyan figure in its advertising. There may have once been a real woodsman named Paul Bunyan. But it was through the imagination of storytellers that he became a legendary hero.

Too Big for Maine

Paul Bunyan was born in Maine, and he wasn't your average baby. The infant rolled around in his sleep so much that he knocked down trees for four miles around. The government told his folks they'd have to keep Paul still or move him away.

So Paul's father cut down some tall trees and built a boat shaped like a cradle. Then he firmly anchored the boat off the coast.

Paul slept there happily for some time. The rolling seas rocked him, and the gulls sang him lullabies.

But one night Paul had a bad dream. He tossed and turned and set his cradle rocking really hard. With every rock, a larger wave arose. Finally a 75-foot tidal wave roared up on shore. Several villages were washed away. The navy had to blast away on its guns to wake the baby and stop the destruction.

"That baby's dangerous!" cried the citizens of Maine. "Get him out of here!"

Paul's mother and father were proud of their child and his enormous strength. But they could see the time had come to move on. So they packed up and headed for Minnesota. There they taught Paul to be a fine young man. They wanted him to be honest and kind, as well as big and strong.

"Never pick on anyone who isn't your own size," Paul's mother told him. But since there wasn't anyone Paul's size anywhere, he never got into trouble.

Paul's father taught him the ways of the forest. He became the best hunter, fisherman, and mountain climber around. He also became the best cutter of trees. And there were plenty of trees to be cut in those

Paul Bunyan

days. Houses, schools, and churches were being built all over the land.

Before long, all the woodsmen knew Paul's cry. "T-I-M-B-E-R-R-R!" he'd roar. The lumberjacks would turn and see Paul standing there with his legs spread wide. He'd be swinging his huge ax in a wide circle. With every swing, a hundred trees would topple.

1. Where was Paul Bunyan born?
2. What happened when baby Paul had a bad dream?
3. Why did Paul never get into trouble as a young man?

Babe, the Blue Ox

Cutting down trees was just part of the lumbering business. Fallen trees then had to be hauled to the river and floated downstream to the sawmills. But Paul got tired of carrying big bundles of trees under his arms. He decided he needed some help.

While Paul was looking for a helper, the Winter of the Blue Snow hit Minnesota. Nobody had ever seen anything like it before. And nobody's seen anything like it since. But blue snow did fall that year.

Paul was out walking one afternoon when he came across a very large snow drift. He tried to wade through it. But then he bumped into a solid blue wall.

Suddenly the wall moved. It heaved and shook, and blue snow flew off it in every direction. This wasn't a wall at all. It was a huge blue ox! Its hair was exactly the same color as the snow. Two blue ears twitched curiously, and two gentle blue eyes stared up at Paul. Although the ox was very large, Paul could see that it was still a calf. Actually, the calf had once been white. Standing around in the freezing blue snow had turned it blue.

"Oh, you beautiful blue babe!" Paul cried. He rubbed the calf's soft nose. When Paul headed back to the lumber camp, the ox followed behind him. In finding Babe, the blue ox, Paul had found the finest helper a lumberjack could want.

Paul and Babe worked the forests of Minnesota and Wisconsin together. Babe was the only animal who could match Paul in energy and strength. By the time he grew to full size, Babe was too large to fit on any scale. The loggers say he stood 42 ax handles tall. Whenever Babe needed new shoes, another iron mine had to be dug. Ole the blacksmith would sink in the ground to his knees carrying just one of the shoes.

Babe could drag 640 acres of trees in a single haul. And he was a great help in other ways as well. If a logging road was too crooked, Paul would just hitch Babe to one end of it. Then he'd whisper in his ear, "Come on, Babe!" The great ox would lean into the job and pull the road straight.

4. How did Babe get to be blue?
5. How tall did the loggers say Babe stood?
6. What would Paul Bunyan do when a logging road was too crooked?

Supper Time

Paul had a crew of seven axmen and one errand boy. They liked each other and worked well together. But they did have one problem. It's well known that lumbermen can eat like crazy. Keeping even a regular crew fed is no small matter. But when you throw in Paul and Babe, you've got yourself quite a task.

The lumbermen's favorite foods were biscuits and pancakes. Even Babe was crazy about pancakes. But Big Joe, the cook, had trouble cooking up enough of them. "I need a bigger griddle!" he told Paul one day.

So Paul went off to the iron works and ordered a gigantic griddle. "Make it so big I won't be able to see across it on a foggy day," he said.

When the griddle was ready, Paul flipped it up on its side. He rolled it back to camp like a silver dollar. Then he dropped the griddle down over a huge hole in which a fire was already burning.

Next Paul strapped slabs of bacon to the feet of some of his men. They went skating over the griddle to get it greased and ready for Big Joe's batter. Soon pancakes were bubbling on the griddle. Babe stood back and waited to gulp down a wagonload.

7. What were the lumbermen's favorite foods?
8. How did Paul get the giant griddle back to camp?
9. How did Paul get the giant griddle greased for pancake batter?

Paul's Biggest Job

A letter from the king of Sweden sent Paul on the biggest job he'd ever tackled.

Paul and his crew were just finishing a logging job in Minnesota when he received the letter.

"The king wants to send some Swedes over here to raise wheat," Paul told his men. "He says they need open fertile land. He'll pay us in silver and gold if we can clear a place for them.

"I think the perfect place for the Swedes would be North Dakota," Paul continued. "With Babe's help, we can have the land cleared in no time."

So Paul, Babe, and the rest of the crew moved their camp to North Dakota. After they had felled the last tree, Paul stepped back and looked out over the land. But the big man frowned. Tree stumps were sticking up everywhere.

"This won't do at all!" Paul cried. He was so upset that he pounded one of the stumps with his fist. It sank six feet into the ground.

"All right!" Paul shouted. He then asked Ole to make him a giant hammer. Then Paul hammered every stump into the ground. Soon the whole state was pounded smooth. Even today it's hard to find a tree stump in North Dakota.

10. *From whom did Paul get an important letter?*
11. *What state did Paul decide to clear for the Swedes?*
12. *What did Paul do with the tree stumps that were sticking up everywhere?*

In the West

After Paul had cleared North Dakota, he turned westward. "I wonder what lies out there," he whispered to Babe.

Paul said good-bye to his friends, and then he and Babe set out for the Pacific Ocean. They traveled through Washington, Oregon, and California.

Babe knocked out some passes in the Cascade Mountains. Paul built one lumber camp after another. They logged tall Douglas firs and redwoods so wide it took a day to walk around them.

Now there are different reports of Paul and Babe's later years. Some folks say they both died on the job. But others say they never stopped working at all.

There have been reports of Paul and Babe clearing land in Alaska. And there are also stories that put the two of them at the North Pole. These stories claim they've been helping Santa Claus build sleighs. But what most lumberjacks say is simply that they sorely miss Paul Bunyan and Babe the blue ox.

13. What states did Paul and Babe travel through after they left North Dakota?
14. What kind of trees did they log there?
15. What do some stories say that Paul and Babe have been doing at the North Pole?

John Henry

> *In the 1820s there were no railroads in America. By 1900, though, the country was crisscrossed with 193,000 miles of track. The rapid build-up of the railroads was exciting and romantic. And the rugged men who laid the ribbons of track that the steam engines ran along made perfect heroes.*
>
> *John Henry was the son of a slave. He had no wealth or education. But people still sing ballads about this heroic worker who helped build a nation.*

John Henry and His Hammer

When John Henry was born, the moon moved backward in the sky and the Mississippi flowed upstream. But as soon as he uttered his first cry, the moon and the river resumed their normal courses. The infant smiled at his parents and reached for a hammer that was hanging on the wall of their cabin. Then he took down the hammer and waved it like a rattle.

While other children played hide-and-seek, John Henry played with his hammer. His father made him a set of wooden pegs, and he spent hours pounding the pegs into the ground. When he was old enough to pick cotton, John Henry outworked all the other slave children.

The Civil War came when he was still a boy. John Henry watched southern soldiers board trains that would take them to fight the armies of the North. To him those trains were magic. The railroad seemed the most exciting thing in the world.

"I'm going to work for the railroad one day," he told his father. "I'm going to be a steel-driving man!"

When the war was over, many black people continued farming. But John Henry had a different idea.

"I had a dream last night," he told his father. "I dreamed I was swinging a mighty hammer. When that hammer hit a spike, the sky lit up with sparks! I'm going to get a job laying track for the railroad. I was born with a hammer in my hand, and I'm bound to die with a hammer in my hand, too!"

John Henry left home and traveled until he found a gang of men building a railroad. He watched the men drive steel spikes into wooden ties to hold the rails in place. As he listened to the clanging of the hammers, he felt his heart beat to their rhythm.

John Henry walked up to the foreman. "I'm a steel-driving man," he said.

The foreman stared at him as if he were somewhat crazy. "You ever done any railroad work?" he asked.

"No," said John Henry. "But just give me a chance, and I'll show you what I can do."

The foreman looked at John Henry's powerful arms. He shrugged and said, "Okay, I'll give you a try." He called one of his crew over to set a spike.

John Henry rubbed his hands together and picked up a long hammer. He swung it high over his head, and smiled. Then he brought the hammer down squarely on the head of the spike. The steel smoked, and before anyone could blink, John Henry had the hammer in the air again. Then he brought it back down and pounded the spike all the way into the tie.

For a moment there was silence. Then one man said, "No one's ever driven a spike *that* quickly!"

The foreman clapped John Henry on the back. "Well! Whoever you are," he said, "you're hired!"

So that's how John Henry became a steel-driver. Before long, everyone who knew about railroading knew about John Henry.

John Henry

He could swing his heavy hammer all day without rest. He could pound spikes faster than anybody thought possible. Why, some days water had to be poured on the tracks just to keep them from catching fire.

1. *What did John Henry play with when he was a boy?*
2. *What did the railroad foreman see that made him decide to give John Henry a chance?*
3. *Why did the foreman hire John Henry on the spot?*

The Race

John Henry was happy when he was swinging his hammer, and his home life was pretty good, too. He married a woman named Polly Ann, and they had two fine children, a boy and a girl.

Polly Ann often brought the children to see their father work. They'd clap and cheer and watch him hammer all day without missing a stroke.

Now John Henry had always claimed he'd been born with a hammer in his hand and that he'd die that way, too. Sad to say, John Henry was right.

In 1870, John Henry was working on the Chesapeake and Ohio Railroad. The C&O was drilling the Big Bend Tunnel through a mountain in West Virginia. At this same time, a machine called the steam drill was being developed.

One day a fellow came into camp boasting about the drill. "It can drive through rock faster than a whole crew of men!" he said.

"I don't need any drill," said the C&O foreman. "I've got John Henry. He can out-drill any machine ever made!"

"Would you like to put a little bet on that?" asked the stranger.

Now the foreman wouldn't make a bet without first talking to John Henry. "Are you willing to race a steam drill?" he asked.

John Henry gripped the handle of his hammer. His muscles swelled. "I'll beat that drill or die trying," he said.

Polly Ann tried to talk John Henry out of the race. Just the thought of it made her shiver.

"Don't you worry, honey," said John Henry on the morning of the race. "I'll be back home just as soon as I beat that machine."

John Henry felt confident as he stood ready for the race. He lifted his hammer, and the foreman gave the signal to start.

Clang! went his hammer, and *bang!* went the steam drill as both tore into the rock.

John Henry worked steadily until he heard someone shout, "The drill's ahead!" John Henry swung faster and faster with every ounce of his strength.

By nightfall, his mouth was set in a hard line and sweat was pouring down his face. But still he pounded and pounded.

At last the foreman cried, "Time's up! The race is over!"

The judges ran forward to measure the holes in the rock. They found that John Henry had gone 14 feet into the mountain. The steam drill had only gone 9 feet.

"You won, John Henry!" the foreman shouted. Everyone cheered and called him a great hero.

But something was wrong. Though the steam drill had stopped, there was still a whirring sound in John Henry's ears. He shook his head, but the sound wouldn't go away. Then John Henry looked off into the distance. Though it was dark now, a fierce light glowed behind his eyes. He shook his head again. Then he staggered and fell.

John Henry died that night. His friends gave his hammer to Polly Ann. But before they could do so, they had to pry it from John Henry's hand.

In time the steam drill took over all the steel-driving. But everyone knew it could never do as good a job as John Henry had. The race at Big Bend had proven that.

4. *What did John Henry race against?*
5. *Who won the race?*
6. *What happened to John Henry after the race?*

Blackbeard

> From colonial days come legends of pirates and hidden treasure. The bandits of the high seas raided merchant ships all along the Atlantic coast. They stalked the waters from Maine to the West Indies. Pirating promised easy money.
>
> In most stories, the pirates were shown to be cruel and ruthless men. In others they were pictured as glamorous rebel-heroes. Edward Teach, better known as Blackbeard, ran his pirate ship out of the Bahamas and North Carolina. Blackbeard was a villain through and through.

The Devil's Twin

While his real name was Edward Teach, it was easy to see why he was called Blackbeard the Pirate. He'd begun growing his beard when he was still in his teens. By the time he was a man, it reached his waist. The whiskers were black as midnight, and he wore them in pigtails tied with ribbons. There was always a mad twinkle in his glowering bloodshot eyes.

Blackbeard was known to mix rum with

gunpowder and then set the brew on fire. He'd drink it while it was still in flames. With the smoke and fire rising around his face, Blackbeard looked like the devil's twin.

Blackbeard and his band sailed the Atlantic coast. He was always being chased by honest sailors, sea captains, and the government. But that didn't stop him from robbing, looting, and murdering.

Blackbeard showed his victims little mercy. When he boarded a ship, he expected its crew and passengers to follow his orders. Usually, seeing his savage face, his three pistol belts, and the crew behind him, they did what they were told. But occasionally a bold prisoner would fail to obey him. One man foolishly refused to give up a diamond ring that he was wearing. So Blackbeard simply chopped the ring from his hand, finger and all.

1. *What was Blackbeard's real name?*
2. *How did Blackbeard wear his waist-length black beard?*
3. *What would Blackbeard often do that made him look like the devil's twin?*

Blackbeard's Last Battle

One day Blackbeard and his men were sailing off the North Carolina coast, searching for their next victim.

"There's a fine mechant ship in the area," said Blackbeard. "She's full of silks and gold. Keep a look-out, mates. We'll feed the crew to the sharks and make the cargo our own!"

Soon Blackbeard saw sails on the horizon. With his eyes fixed on the sails, he didn't notice a sloop coming up from behind.

The master of the approaching sloop was Lieutenant Robert Maynard of the Royal Navy. Maynard had sworn to capture Blackbeard or die trying. Now his sloop was gaining on Blackbeard's ship. As they sailed into Ocracoke Inlet, the royal sloop overtook the pirate boat.

Maynard and his men fearlessly boarded the pirate ship, their pistols and cutlasses in hand.

"Blackbeard! Prepare to fight for your life!" Maynard shouted.

The slashing and shooting that followed soon had the decks running with blood. After many men had been killed, Blackbeard and Maynard faced each other.

Blackbeard waved his cutlass in the air. The sun glittered on its curved blade. The

Blackbeard

pirate roared, angry as a bull. Just as the two men lunged at each other, the sun shone directly in Blackbeard's eyes. Maynard saw that his enemy was blinded, and he took the advantage. His saber flashed, and off flew the pirate's head! It sailed through the air, pigtails flying, and landed on the bloody deck.

Now that *should* have been the end of Blackbeard. But the villain's body leaped up, ran around the deck, and dove into the sea. Then the headless corpse swam three times around the ship with strong steady strokes.

At last Blackbeard's body went down, and the sea closed over it. Lieutenant Maynard had Blackbeard's head mounted on the mast of the ship. Its pigtailed beard fluttering in the wind was a warning to all who held thoughts of piracy.

Some people believe Blackbeard is still haunting Ocracoke Inlet. Fishermen report seeing a headless corpse swimming in the water. And other folks say they've seen it come ashore and tramp up and down the beaches. They say Blackbeard is looking for his head.

4. *What did Blackbeard's body do after he was killed?*
5. *What happened during the fight that gave Maynard the advantage?*
6. *What did Maynard mount on the mast of his ship?*

Jean Lafitte

Long fingers of water reach inland from the Gulf of Mexico. They tangle and twine with branches of the Mississippi River. The resulting maze of waterways is known as the Louisiana bayous. Only the most skilled boatmen can find their way among them.

At one time, these marshlands made fine hideouts for outlaws. The Frenchman Jean Lafitte was the leader of a band of gulf pirates. Lafitte sailed from France to New Orleans in about 1809. It was there that his legend began.

The Pirates of Barataria Bay

Barataria Bay is on the Louisiana gulf coast. A rugged band of outlaws once camped there and made their living raiding Spanish ships. The Baratarian band flew the flag of Cartagena, a city in South America. Since Cartagena was at war with Spain, these men claimed the right to attack Spanish ships. They called themselves "privateers," but most people just called them pirates.

The leader of the Baratarians was a tall fellow who would dress in fine clothes and spend most of his time in New Orleans. His name was Jean Lafitte.

Lafitte sold his stolen goods in a fine shop on Royal Street. To the wealthy ladies and gentlemen of the city, Lafitte was a pirate. But they still bought silks, velvet, and jewelry from him.

In 1812, the United States went to war with Britain. British troops planned to seize New Orleans, and U.S. President Andrew Jackson knew they had to be stopped. Now Lafitte may have been an outlaw, but he felt loyal to America. He offered his ship and crew to join the fight against the British.

"I'll never have pirates fighting for me!" said Jackson. But as the British approached New Orleans, Jackson saw that the American army was badly outnumbered. Desperate for help, he accepted the offer. Lafitte's crew sent the redcoats running.

"They fight like devils!" said Jackson. "Like devils and wildcats!"

Lafitte helped save New Orleans. But he had trouble accepting the honors that were then heaped upon him. City leaders invited him to parties and balls. But Lafitte thought they were laughing at him and calling him a pirate behind his back.

Lafitte left New Orleans and went to Galveston Island, off the coast of Texas. There he gathered a new band of outlaws and started pirating in earnest. He attacked any ship from any nation, even American vessels. It was said that he buried chests of stolen treasure all along the coasts of Texas and Louisiana. Lafitte himself boasted that he'd buried enough money to build a solid gold bridge across the Mississippi River.

1. Why did Jean Lafitte's band raid Spanish ships?
2. How did Jean Lafitte sell his stolen goods?
3. Where did Lafitte go after leaving New Orleans?

Lafitte's Ghost

There are many tales about Jean Lafitte's last days. Some say he died in bed of a tropical fever. Others say a storm at sea took his life. There are stories that describe a final bloody duel.

The most famous legend of Jean Lafitte takes place after his death. It is the tale of the pirate's ghost.

It seems that Lafitte had a conscience. He knew he'd committed many wrongs in his life. When he died, his ghost would not rest until the wrongs had been set right.

The ghost of Jean Lafitte dwelt in a large deserted house on Galveston Bay. It was near the town of La Porte. Hidden in that house was a chest filled with treasure. Lafitte's mournful ghost had a mission. It wanted to find a man who would use the treasure unselfishly. The ghost waited and watched for someone who wouldn't spend a penny on himself but would only give to others.

One misty evening in 1880, a gentleman went riding down a little-used road on the Galveston coast. He was an elderly fellow who'd been an army major during the Civil War. Daylight was fading, and the major was tired. He squinted and made out the shape of a house in the distance.

The major rode up to the ramshackle house and got down from his horse. He took his saddle and blanket and went to the front door. He knocked on the door, but no one came to answer it. He called out loudly but still got no response.

The major made his way to the back of the house. There he found a broken window.

He climbed through it into a large gloomy room. There was nothing in the room but a stack of wood piled beside a fireplace.

The major got a fire going and then spread out his blanket. He lay down and soon fell sound asleep.

But he didn't stay asleep for long. He awoke suddenly, feeling that he wasn't alone. The major opened his eyes to find a man standing over him. The man was staring at him with a fixed gaze. His eyes burned steadily but held no menace. They seemed to be pleading.

The figure motioned for the major to follow him. The major did as he was asked, for he seemed to have lost all free will. The figure floated rather than walked. The major then knew he was following a ghost.

The ghost led the way to a smaller room that was also empty of furniture. He stopped and turned toward the major.

"Here," the ghost said, "lies buried more treasure than is good for any man. Dig it up and it's yours. However, you must use the treasure unselfishly. You may not spend a penny on yourself. If you do, you'll be very sorry. Do you accept this offer?"

"Yes," said the major, feeling it was what he was supposed to say. The figure disappeared. The major hurried back to the room he'd been sleeping in. He heaped more wood on the fire, wrapped the blanket tightly around him, and stretched out again.

The major thought about his ghostly visitor. Had he really seen it? Probably so, he thought. But that meant that the offer was real as well. And how could a man own a treasure and not spend a penny on himself? The major thought himself a good man, but after all, he was only human. And no one could be *totally* unselfish!

The major had just dozed off again when the specter reappeared.

"I need your help," it begged. "Take the treasure! Only then can you remove the guilt I feel."

The ghost led the major back to the smaller room. This time a large oak chest stood open on the floor. The major gasped. The chest was filled with coins, watches, rings, and necklaces.

"Take it!" the ghost commanded. "Don't force me to come again!" Then he vanished as he had before.

The major stumbled back to the room with the fireplace. He grabbed his blanket and saddle, rushed from the house, and mounted his horse. Across the chilly bay, a ray of light was just then appearing. Never did a man more welcome the dawn! The major rode off as fast as he could.

They say Lafitte's ghost still haunts that lonely house. On stormy nights, the winds that blow around the house carry a cry of despair: "Is there no one who will ease my soul's burden?"

4. What made the major wake up after he had fallen asleep?
5. What treasure was in the chest?
6. Why do you think the major decided not to take the treasure?

Jesse James

The Kansas-Missouri border was a restless place before, during, and after the Civil War. Slavery was the main issue, but people were fighting over all kinds of things. Before long, most folks couldn't say what the problem was. But there was lots of hatred and lots of killing.

It was during this time that Jesse James joined up with a Confederate force led by "Bloody" Bill Anderson. The Anderson gang wasn't "regular" army. It was made up of tough rebels who specialized in bloody sneak attacks.

When the Civil War ended in 1865, Jesse went off with his brother Frank. They gathered a band of outlaws, including their cousins, the Younger brothers.

But Jesse James, it seems, wasn't all bad. "There was good in him too," some folks insisted. No doubt, it was the good and bad all rolled together that made Jesse James a colorful figure in American folklore.

The Laughing Bandit

Jesse James robbed banks and trains and was known to enjoy a good laugh.

On a hot afternoon in July of 1871, the James gang rode into Corydon, Iowa, to rob its bank.

At the same time, a political rally was being held in town. Just about everyone in Corydon had gathered at the square and was listening to speeches. A single cashier remained in the bank.

When the outlaws walked in with bandannas tied across their faces, the bank teller threw up his hands. The gang left the bank with $45,000.

Jesse James felt so good he decided to have a little fun. He walked over to the square and began heckling the man who was speaking. He kept trying to interrupt him, and folks repeatedly told Jesse to be quiet.

Finally, the speaker said, "You, sir! What do you have to say that's so important you won't let me finish my speech?"

"I'm sorry to interrupt you," Jesse said. "But I think your bank's just been robbed. Maybe you'd better look into it." Jesse laughed and ran to his horse. Then he and his boys dashed away in a cloud of dust.

Now, it might seem strange that no one in the square had recognized Jesse James. But there weren't many folks anywhere who knew what the James boys looked like.

Jesse, on the other hand, always made sure he knew by sight anyone who might be after him.

One day in Louisville, Jesse happened to see a fellow named Bligh. This fellow had been on Jesse's trail for some time.

Jesse followed Bligh into a saloon and started a conversation. Soon he brought up the subject of a recent robbery. "I read in the papers that it was the James boys who robbed that bank," Jesse said.

Bligh struck his fist on the bar. "I'd like to see that Jesse James before I die," he said angrily.

A few days later, Bligh received a postcard. It mentioned the conversation in the Louisville saloon.

"You have seen Jesse James," the card said. "Now you can go ahead and die!" The card was signed, "Your friend, Jesse James."

1. *While the James gang was robbing the bank in Corydon, where were most of the townspeople?*
2. *Where did Jesse James meet up with Bligh?*
3. *What did Jesse send to Bligh a few days after they talked?*

The Stories They Told

Although he was an outlaw, storytellers loved to point out Jesse's good side. They say he was fearless. Once Jesse was almost captured after robbing a bank in Alabama.

Lawmen were on his heels, and they chased him to the edge of a high cliff. Jesse rode his horse right off the cliff and plunged into the river. Unfortunately, the horse was killed. But Jesse escaped.

Jesse was also said to be generous. "He was great about helping the poor," one of his old neighbors recalled. "When we were sick, Jesse would fetch the doctor. He'd even stay a while and help take care of our animals."

Jesse got a reputation for helping the poor and tricking the rich. One summer's day he was riding down a lonely road when he heard cries coming from a shack. Jesse investigated and found an old woman whose landlord had ordered her out of her house.

"I can't pay the mortgage," the old woman cried. "My landlord is heartless! He won't give me a single day longer to come up with the cash!"

Jesse gave the woman the exact amount of money she needed. He got back on

Wanted: Jesse James

his horse and rode a short ways down the road. Then he stopped, hid in a stand of trees, and waited.

Now the landlord was very surprised when the woman gave him the cash for her mortgage. But he took it, said nothing, and started off down the road. When he came to the stand of trees, out rode Jesse. A bandanna covered his face. He pointed his gun at the landlord.

"Give me your money!" Jesse demanded.

The landlord handed over the money Jesse had given the woman.

"Not a bad deal," Jesse later laughed. "I lent out my money, made someone happy, got back every penny, and had myself a grand old time!"

But Jesse's wild ways finally caught up with him. A fellow can't live forever with a price on his head—especially not when it's $10,000. That's what the government was offering for his capture, dead or alive. Someone was bound to make a claim for that reward. It turned out to be a man named Robert Ford.

Folks say Ford gained Jesse's trust and joined the James gang. Then he killed Jesse by shooting him in the back of the head. It happened right in Jesse's own house.

4. What happened when lawmen chased Jesse James to the edge of a cliff?
5. How did Jesse get back the money he had given the woman?
6. How did Jesse James meet his end?

Rip Van Winkle

> *Rip Van Winkle is a character made famous in a story written by Washington Irving. Irving was interested in the history of the Dutch in upstate New York. He traveled the countryside listening to the Dutch farmers' colorful folktales. In 1819, Irving published the tale of Rip Van Winkle in a book called* The Sketch Book. *The story of Rip Van Winkle has since become one of the most popular American legends.*

An Autumn Stroll

In a little village on the Hudson River there lived a fellow named Rip Van Winkle.

It would be harsh to say that Rip was lazy. But he did shy away from most sorts of work. He preferred to spend his days fishing and hunting or merely tramping through the woods. If left to it, he would have whittled away his life in such pursuits. But his wife would have nothing of it. She continually nagged him about his idleness.

Driven from the house by his wife's badgering, Rip often made his way to the village inn. One day his wife went there after him. Rip was drinking and swapping stories with his pals. Dame Van Winkle shouted at them all. She angrily wagged her finger in their faces. Rip was embarrassed. He fled the inn and escaped to the woods.

It was a fine autumn day, so Rip began climbing through the hills. In time he came to one of the highest parts of the Catskill Mountains. Tired from climbing, he sat down to rest. Rip knew he'd come a long way and that it would be dark by the time he got home. He shuddered to think of the greeting he'd get from his wife.

He was about to start down the hill when he heard a voice. "Rip Van Winkle!" it cried. Then he saw a strange figure climbing over the rocks.

"Perhaps he needs help," Rip thought. He walked toward the stranger.

Rip was surprised at the fellow's appearance. He was short and squarely built. He had thick bushy hair and a grizzled beard, and he seemed rather old. He was carrying a keg on his shoulder. The man motioned for Rip to help him with his load.

Rip was a rather shy fellow, but he was always willing to lend a hand. He took hold of one end of the keg. Then he and the stranger followed a narrow gully until they came to a hollow in the hills.

The sight that greeted Rip in that hollow was indeed a wonder. A group of odd-looking men were playing nine-pins, a game much like bowling. They were dressed in old-fashioned costumes of bright, mismatched colors. One man had a bushy beard, a broad face, and small piggish eyes. Little could be seen of another man's face other than a huge nose. This man's head was topped by a large floppy white hat.

These fellows had a serious manner about them even though they were playing a game. The only sounds to be heard were those of the balls striking the pins. That noise echoed through the mountains like peals of thunder. The game stopped only when players went to drink from the keg Rip had helped deliver.

Rip watched for a while. The men were odd, but they seemed to mean him no harm. At last Rip relaxed. Finding himself thirsty, he went over to the keg and took a drink from it.

"What an excellent beverage!" Rip declared. He took another drink, and then another. After several more trips to the keg, Rip's head began to nod. His eyes grew heavy. So Rip sat down against a tree and fell into a deep sleep.

Rip Van Winkle

1. Why did Rip Van Winkle escape to the woods that day?
2. What did the strange old man want Rip to help him carry?
3. What were the men in the hollow playing?

Awakening

When Rip awoke, he found himself on the green hill where he'd first seen the man with the keg. Rip rubbed his eyes. It was a bright, sunny morning.

"Surely," Rip thought, "I haven't slept here all night! It must have been the drink." Rip shook his head. "Oh, Dame Van Winkle is going to be very angry, indeed! What excuse shall I make?"

As Rip rose to stand, he found that his legs were very stiff. In fact, he couldn't remember a time when the act of standing took so much effort. With some difficulty, Rip made his way toward his village.

When he got there, he saw a number of people, but he didn't recognize any of them. Rip stared, and the people stared back. When men looked at Rip, they reached up and stroked their chins. Rip reached up to touch his own chin. "What's this?" he cried aloud. Rip's beard was at least a foot long.

As he made his way through the streets, Rip saw that the entire village had changed. Suddenly it had grown larger. Familiar buildings seemed to have disappeared overnight.

At last he turned the corner of his own street. He walked to his house and found it empty and uncared for. Weeds had grown as high as the windows. Grass grew from cracks in the walls.

Rip turned and hurried to the village inn. It was gone! A large hotel stood in its place.

A crowd now gathered around the confused Rip Van Winkle. People pointed at his tattered clothing and his long beard.

"Who are you?" one man asked.

"Why, I am a native of this village," Rip answered. "And I'm a loyal subject of the king of England!"

"The king?" cried the man. Then other voices began shouting. "He's a traitor! The man's a Tory! He's a spy! Away with him."

Poor Rip assured them he meant no harm. "I'm merely looking for my neighbors," he said.

"And who might they be?" a villager asked him.

Rip thought for a moment. "Well, there's Nicholas Vedder. Where is he?"

No one seemed to know the name. Then one old man said, "Nicholas Vedder? Why, he's been dead for 18 years!"

Rip felt dizzy. What had happened to his friends, to his village, to his life?

Just then a young woman pressed through the crowd to get a look at the gray-bearded man.

"Hush, Rip," she said to the child who tugged at her skirt.

The child's name caught Rip's attention. And there was something familiar about the woman's voice. "Who are you, good woman?" he asked.

"Judith Gardiner," she replied.

"And your father's name?"

"Ah, my poor father," the woman sadly replied. "His name was Rip Van Winkle. But it's been 20 years since he left home. No one's seen or heard from him since."

Rip's voice quivered as he asked, "And where is your mother?"

"Oh, she died. She broke a blood vessel while arguing with a peddler."

Rip sighed. Then he exclaimed, "I am your father! Young Rip once, Old Rip now!"

All listened in amazement to Rip's story. He described how the last 20 years had passed for him as a single night.

Rip's daughter took him home to live with her. She had a snug home and a cheery farmer for a husband. Rip was happy now, for no one expected an old man to work. He found himself a sunny place on a bench outside the hotel door. There people would stop to talk. They honored Rip as the wise old man of the village.

Rip told his story to every stranger who came to the hotel. And many who heard it shared the same hope. They wished they could meet those strange-looking men in the mountains and drink from their wonderful keg.

4. What had grown on Rip's chin while he was sleeping?
5. What was the name of Rip Van Winkle's daughter?
6. How had Rip's wife died?

The Witches of Windham

> *The early Puritan settlers in New England built their villages on the edges of dark forests. There they listened to the warnings of their grim ministers. "Beware the devil. His spirits of darkness are among us."*
>
> *The early New Englanders imagined all sorts of evil. They saw evil in the black cat hiding in the shadows. They saw evil in the owl hooting in the trees at night. When crops failed or sickness struck, the devil was blamed. In a climate of fear and superstition, stories of demons and witches flourished.*

The people of New England were seeing witches everywhere. They saw them riding broomsticks through the sky on stormy nights. They saw them dancing in the graveyards. They heard them clattering in their chimneys. When firelight flickered weirdly on their windowpanes, people saw witches' faces peering into their homes. The witches were turning themselves into crows and cawing in the treetops. With invisible hands, they were pricking people with pins.

It went on like this for years.

On a summer's night in 1758, the people of Windham, Connecticut, had a particularly interesting experience. It happened at a time when two men, Dyer and Elderkin, were running against each other for public office. The day had been filled with speeches and arguments. Half the town supported Colonel Dyer. The other half wanted Mr. Elderkin to win the upcoming election.

The townspeople were all in their beds when the air became filled with a shrill screeching and a thunderous booming. The sounds seemed to be coming from the edge of town.

"The witches are coming!" the people cried. "They've mounted their broomsticks and are coming to get us!"

The people barred their windows. They hid under their covers.

All night long the terrible sounds filled the air. At a certain point, people began to hear words in the noise.

"Colonel Dyer! Colonel Dyer!"

"Elderkin too! Elderkin too!"

Obviously the witches were arguing over the election. Trembling in their beds, the Dyer supporters wondered what terrible spells the Elderkin witches would cast on them. And the Elderkin voters shivered in fear of the witches on Dyer's side.

Only when dawn lit the sky did anyone venture outside. Then a party of heavily armed men made their way to the edge of town. There they found hundreds of frogs lying dead by a ditch.

The weather had been unusually hot and dry. Most of the ponds had dried up. The frogs had been battling over a small, still-damp ditch. The noise the people had taken for the din of witches had been the sound of the struggling frogs. Small frogs had piped, "Colonel Dyer! Colonel Dyer!" Deep-voiced bullfrogs had boomed, "Elderkin too! Elderkin too!"

And there stood the Windham warriors, holding their muskets and axes and staring at a pile of dead frogs.

Word spread about the night the witches came to Windham. It became quite a joke. But people began to think. If Windham's witches were actually frogs, then maybe cats were only cats. Maybe crows in cornfields were only looking for corn.

After the Windham witch scare, people were a little less quick to cry "witch" at every unusual turn.

1. Which two men were running against each other for public office?
2. Who did the people think were making the terrible noises?
3. As it turned out, what was really making the sounds?

Flight

Africans who were brought to America as slaves were not permitted to learn to read or write. But they recorded their pain, anger, and hope in stories and songs. This tale recalls an African myth that tells of days when people could fly.

Long, long ago, when the world was new, human beings and animals were not like they are today. In those days, animals could talk like people. And people could fly like birds. Things changed, of course. But even as late as slavery days, there were still some people who remembered how to fly.

These people looked just like everyone else. And when one of them turned up on a certain American cotton plantation, no one guessed he was different.

The owner of this plantation was a cruel man. He worked his slaves for long hours in the burning sun. He demanded more from them than they were able to give. One by one, they all died. So the owner bought new slaves. He found a group of men and women who had just arrived from Africa and put them to work in his cotton fields.

Plantation work

Among these new slaves was a young woman who had recently given birth. She was still weak but was sent directly to the fields anyway. She carried her newborn baby in a cloth sling on her hip. When the baby cried, she would speak to it softly in words the plantation foreman couldn't understand. Then the child would be still, and the woman would return to picking cotton.

But one day, in the heat of the afternoon sun, the woman stumbled and fell. The foreman hit her with his whip until she got up. She then turned to a man who worked beside her. Although this man was the oldest of the slaves, he was also tall and strong. The woman said something to the old man, and he answered her. But the foreman didn't understand their words. Then the woman went back to work.

Before long, she fell again. Once more the foreman whipped her to her feet. She turned to the tall old man again. "Not yet," he said. So she went back to work.

She fell down a third time. The foreman came running at her with his whip. When she turned to the old man this time, he said, "Yes." Then he raised his arms and said, "Go, daughter. Go!"

With that, she leaped straight into the air. She flew away with her baby tucked on her hip.

The foreman simply refused to believe his eyes. He shouted to the others to get back to work. When they hesitated, he lashed them with his whip. Another slave fell. Then the old man called out in the unknown language. As soon as he spoke, the man who had fallen stood on his feet and laughed. Then he leaped into the air and went flying over the fields.

By this time, the plantation owner had come out to the fields. He was just in time to see a third slave fall. Again, the foreman used his lash. Again, the old man called out. And again, a slave flew away.

"Get the old devil!" the owner cried out. "Get him!"

The foreman ran at the man with his whip. The owner ran at him with a stick. The old man laughed at both of them. Then he spoke some words loudly to the other slaves in the field.

As he spoke, all the people there remembered what they'd forgotten. They recalled the power that had once been theirs. The old man raised his arms, and every man, woman, and child in the field leaped into the air. The old man flew off behind the others. All were lost from sight in the brightness of the sun.

1. What did the plantation owner do when all his slaves died?
2. What did the foreman do every time the young woman fell?
3. What happened after the foreman and the owner ran at the old man?

The Jumping Frog

> *In the 1860s, Mark Twain worked as a reporter in San Francisco. During that time, he became friendly with a gold miner named Jim Gillis. Together they visited mining camps in northern California.*
>
> *It is said that Twain first heard the story of "The Jumping Frog of Calaveras" at Angels Camp. Mark Twain put the story to paper. "The Celebrated Jumping Frog of Calaveras County" became an American legend. Here is a version of that tale.*

One day a stranger appeared at Angels Camp. His pockets jingled, and he said he was a gambler. The stranger talked loudly about his gambling days. But no one ever saw him make a wager.

Pretty soon the men started taunting him. They pushed him to make a bet. Finally the stranger put his hands in his pockets and stuck his chin out with an air of importance.

"I have a frog," he said, "that'll leap farther than any frog you can find!"

The men around him laughed loudly.

"Yes," said the gambler, "and I'll bet money on it."

"Smiley's got a frog," said one of the men. "It's a darn good jumper! I'll bet it can outjump this fellow's frog by a mile!"

"Tell Smiley to bring his frog to the saloon tomorrow," the stranger said. "We'll see who's got the best jumper."

The men found Smiley and told him the news. Smiley's grin was so wide it was plain to see how he'd gotten his name. He got out his frog and held it up for all to see.

"This frog's a champion," he said. "He'll take on *any* challenger!"

After everyone had admired the frog, Smiley put it away. Then he and his pals went out for a night on the town.

Next day, everyone in Angels Camp gathered at the saloon for the contest. The stranger had a frog in a box. Smiley had his frog in a box, too. Both men put their bets down on the bar and set their boxes on the floor behind a white chalk line. Then they opened the boxes. Out came the gambler's frog. Out came Smiley's.

The gambler went first. He whacked a board onto the floor behind his frog to give it a little start. The frog jumped up and traveled forward six feet.

"That's a pretty good jump," said Smiley. He grinned enormously, knowing his own frog could jump a lot farther than that.

Smiley whacked the floor behind his frog. "Jump, frog!" he cried. "Jump!"

Smiley's frog seemed to gather up all its strength. But instead of leaping grandly through the air, it just lurched forward. That frog couldn't have gone more than half a foot at the most.

"Jump, frog!" Smiley shouted. The poor frog struggled forward another few inches. "What's the matter with you?" cried Smiley. "Jump! Jump!"

"That's quite a frog," said the stranger. He laughed as he scooped up the money on the bar. "I guess I'll be on my way now."

"What's wrong with you?" Smiley asked his frog. Then he picked it up in his hands. "Hey, what's this? My frog is mighty heavy!"

"I reckon it would be," said the stranger on his way out. "He ate real well when I fed him that pound of buckshot last night."

1. *What bet did the stranger make?*
2. *Where did the contest take place?*
3. *Why couldn't Smiley's frog jump?*

Pronunciation Guide

> Every effort has been made to present native pronunciations of the unusual names in this book. Sometimes experts differed in their opinions, however, or no pronunciation could be found. Also, certain foreign-language sounds were felt to be unpronounceable by today's readers. In these cases, editorial license was exercised in selecting pronunciations.

Key

Capital letters are used to represent stressed syllables. For example, the word *ugly* would be written here as "UHG lee."

The letter or letters used to show pronunciation have the following sounds:

- **a** as in *map* and *glad*
- **ah** as in *pot* and *cart*
- **aw** as in *fall* and *lost*
- **ch** as in *chair* and *child*
- **e** as in *let* and *care*
- **ee** as in *feet* and *please*
- **ey** as in *play* and *face*
- **g** as in *gold* and *girl*

hy as in *huge* and *humor*
i as in *my* and *high*
ih as in *sit* and *clear*
j as in *jelly* and *gentle*
k as in *skill* and *can*
ky as in *cute*
l as in *long* and *pull*
my as in *mule*
ng as in *sing* and *long*
o as in *slow* and *go*
oo as in *cool* and *move*
ow as in *cow* and *round*
s as in *soon* and *cent*
sh as in *shoe* and *sugar*
th as in *thin* and *myth*
u as in *put* and *look*
uh as in *run* and *up*
y as in *you* and *yesterday*
z as in *zoo* and *pairs*

Guide

adobe: uh DO bee
Alamo: AL uh mo
Barataria Bay: ber uh TER ee uh BEY
bayou: BAH yoo
Bligh: BLI
Bunyan, Paul: BUHN yuhn, PAWL
Calaveras: kal uh VER uhs
Cartagena: kahr tuh HEYN uh

Corydon: KOR ih duhn
Cristobal: krihs TO bahl
Dyer: DI ur
Feboldson, Febold: FEE buhld suhn, FEE bold
Felipa: fe LEEP uh
José: ho SEY
La Porte: lah PORT
Lafitte, Jean: la FEET, ZHAHN
Natchez: NACH ez
Navajo: NAV uh ho
Negrita: ne GREE tuh
Ocracoke: OK ruh kok
Ole: O luh
Pecos Bill: PEY kos BIHL
Pueblo: PWEB lo
Quantrill, William: kwahn TRIHL, WIHL yuhm
Rio Grande: REE o GRAND
Slue-foot Sue: SLOO fut SOO
Tippecanoe: tihp uh kuhn OO
Ute: YOOT
Windham: WIHN duhm